Tao Te Ching

BESTSELLING NON-FICTION

- Gravity by George Gamow
  Sciences/Physics, ISBN: 9789388118705
- How to Develop Self-Confi. and Pub. Speaking by Dale Carnegie
  Mind, Body & Spirit, ISBN: 9789388118286
- How to Stop Worrying and Start Living by Dale Carnegie
  Mind, Body & Spirit, ISBN: 9789387669161
- How to Win Friends and Influence People by Dale Carnegie
  Self Help/General, ISBN: 9789387669178
- Mein Kampf by Adolf Hitler
  Autobiographies/Leaders, ISBN: 9789387669260
- My Experiments with Truth by Mahatma Gandhi
  Autobiographies/Leaders, ISBN: 9789387669277
- Relativity by Albert Einstein
  Sciences/Physics, ISBN: 9789387669185
- The Art of War by Sun Tzu
  Self Help/Success, ISBN: 9789387669321
- The Diary of a Young Girl by Anne Frank
  Autobiographies/Memoirs, ISBN: 9789387669208
- The Magic of Believing by Claudie Bristol
  Religion/Christianity, ISBN: 9789388118217
- The Miracles of Your Mind by Joseph Murphy
  Mind, Body & Spirit, ISBN: 9789387669215
- The Power of Your Subconscious Mind by Joseph Murphy
  Mind, Body & Spirit, ISBN: 9789387669222
- The Richest Man in Babylon by George S. Clason
  Business & Economics, ISBN: 9789388118354
- Think and Grow Rich by Napoleon Hill
  Self Help/Success, ISBN: 9789387669352

Search the book by its ISBN

TAO TE CHING

THE CLASSIC BOOK OF
INTEGRITY AND THE WAY

LAO TZU

GENERAL PRESS

Published by
GENERAL PRESS
4805/24, Fourth Floor, Krishna House
Ansari Road, Daryaganj, New Delhi - 110002
Ph : 011-23282971, 45795759
E-mail : generalpressindia@gmail.com

www.generalpress.in

First Edition : 2022

ISBN : 9789354992629

Published by Azeem Ahmad Khan for General Press

Contents

PART 1

CHAPTER 1

The Tao that can be trodden is not the enduring and unchanging Tao. The name that can be named is not the enduring and unchanging name.

(Conceived of as) having no name, it is the Originator of heaven and earth; (conceived of as) having a name, it is the Mother of all things.

Always without desire we must be found,
If its deep mystery we would sound;
But if desire always within us be,
Its outer fringe is all that we shall see.

Under these two aspects, it is really the same; but as development takes place, it receives the different names. Together we call them the Mystery. Where the Mystery is the deepest is the gate of all that is subtle and wonderful.

CHAPTER 2

All in the world know the beauty of the beautiful, and in doing this they have (the idea of) what ugliness is; they all know the skill of the skilful, and in doing this they have (the idea of) what they want of skill is.

So it is that existence and non-existence give birth the one to (the idea of) the other; that difficulty and ease produce the one (the idea of) the other; that length and shortness fashion out the one the figure of the other; that (the ideas of) height and lowness arise from the contrast of the one with the other; that the musical notes and tones become harmonious through the relation of one with another; and that being before and behind give the idea of one following another.

Therefore the sage manages affairs without doing anything, and conveys his instructions without the use of speech.

All things spring up, and there is not one which declines to show itself; they grow, and there is no claim made for their ownership; they go through their processes, and there is no expectation (of a reward for the results). The work is accomplished, and there is no resting in it (as an achievement).

The work is done, but how no one can see;
'Tis this that makes the power not cease to be.

CHAPTER 3

Not to value and employ men of superior ability is the way to keep the people from rivalry among themselves; not to prize articles which are difficult to procure is the way to keep them from becoming thieves; not to show them what is likely to excite their desires is the way to keep their minds from disorder.

Therefore the sage, in the exercise of his government, empties their minds, fills their bellies, weakens their wills, and strengthens their bones.

He constantly (tries to) keep them without knowledge and without desire, and where there are those who have knowledge, to keep them from presuming to act (on it). When there is this abstinence from action, good order is universal.

CHAPTER 4

The Tao is (like) the emptiness of a vessel; and in our employment of it we must be on our guard against all fulness. How deep and unfathomable it is, as if it were the Honoured Ancestor of all things!

We should blunt our sharp points, and unravel the complications of things; we should attemper our brightness, and bring ourselves into agreement with the obscurity of others. How pure and still the Tao is, as if it would ever so continue!

I do not know whose son it is. It might appear to have been before God.

CHAPTER 5

Heaven and earth do not act from (the impulse of) any wish to be benevolent; they deal with all things as the dogs of grass are dealt with. The sages do not act from (any wish to be) benevolent; they deal with the people as the dogs of grass are dealt with.

May not the space between heaven and earth be compared to a bellows?

'Tis emptied, yet it loses not its power;
'Tis moved again, and sends forth air the more.
Much speech to swift exhaustion lead we see;
Your inner being guard, and keep it free.

CHAPTER 6

The valley spirit dies not, aye the same;
The female mystery thus do we name.
Its gate, from which at first they issued forth,
Is called the root from which grew heaven and earth.
Long and unbroken does its power remain,
Used gently, and without the touch of pain.

CHAPTER 7

Heaven is long-enduring and earth continues long. The reason why heaven and earth are able to endure and continue thus long is because they do not live of, or for, themselves. This is how they are able to continue and endure.

Therefore the sage puts his own person last, and yet it is found in the foremost place; he treats his person as if it were foreign to him, and yet that person is preserved. Is it not because he has no personal and private ends, that therefore such ends are realised?

CHAPTER 8

The highest excellence is like (that of) water. The excellence of water appears in its benefiting all things, and in its occupying, without striving (to the contrary), the low place which all men dislike. Hence (its way) is near to (that of) the Tao.

The excellence of a residence is in (the suitability of) the place; that of the mind is in abysmal stillness; that of associations is in their being with the virtuous; that of government is in its securing good order; that of (the conduct of) affairs is in its ability; and that of (the initiation of) any movement is in its timeliness.

And when (one with the highest excellence) does not wrangle (about his low position), no one finds fault with him.

CHAPTER 9

It is better to leave a vessel unfilled, than to attempt to carry it when it is full. If you keep feeling a point that has been sharpened, the point cannot long preserve its sharpness.

When gold and jade fill the hall, their possessor cannot keep them safe. When wealth and honours lead to arrogancy, this brings its evil on itself. When the work is done, and one's name is becoming distinguished, to withdraw into obscurity is the way of Heaven.

CHAPTER 10

When the intelligent and animal souls are held together in one embrace, they can be kept from separating. When one gives undivided attention to the (vital) breath, and brings it to the utmost degree of pliancy, he can become as a (tender) babe. When he has cleansed away the most mysterious sights (of his imagination), he can become without a flaw.

In loving the people and ruling the state, cannot he proceed without any (purpose of) action? In the opening and shutting of his gates of heaven, cannot he do so as a female bird? While his intelligence reaches in every direction, cannot he (appear to) be without knowledge?

(The Tao) produces (all things) and nourishes them; it produces them and does not claim them as its own; it does all, and yet does not boast of it; it presides over all, and yet does not control them. This is what is called 'The mysterious Quality' (of the Tao).

CHAPTER 11

The thirty spokes unite in the one nave; but it is on the empty space (for the axle), that the use of the wheel depends. Clay is fashioned into vessels; but it is on their empty hollowness, that their use depends. The door and windows are cut out (from the walls) to form an apartment; but it is on the empty space (within), that its use depends. Therefore, what has a (positive) existence serves for profitable adaptation, and what has not that for (actual) usefulness.

CHAPTER 12

Colour's five hues from th' eyes their sight will take;
Music's five notes the ears as deaf can make;
The flavours five deprive the mouth of taste;
The chariot course, and the wild hunting waste
Make mad the mind; and objects rare and strange,
Sought for, men's conduct will to evil change.

Therefore the sage seeks to satisfy (the craving of) the belly, and not the (insatiable longing of the) eyes. He puts from him the latter, and prefers to seek the former.

CHAPTER 13

Favour and disgrace would seem equally to be feared; honour and great calamity, to be regarded as personal conditions (of the same kind).

What is meant by speaking thus of favour and disgrace? Disgrace is being in a low position (after the enjoyment of favour). The getting that (favour) leads to the apprehension (of losing it), and the losing it leads to the fear of (still greater calamity):—this is what is meant by saying that favour and disgrace would seem equally to be feared. And what is meant by saying that honour and great calamity are to be (similarly) regarded as personal conditions? What makes me liable to great calamity is my having the body (which I call myself); if I had not the body, what great calamity could come to me?

Therefore he who would administer the kingdom, honouring it as he honours his own person, may be employed to govern it, and he who would administer it with the love which he bears to his own person may be entrusted with it.

CHAPTER 14

We look at it, and we do not see it, and we name it 'the Equable.' We listen to it, and we do not hear it, and we name it 'the Inaudible.' We try to grasp it, and do not get hold of it, and we name it 'the Subtle.' With these three qualities, it cannot be made the subject of description; and hence we blend them together and obtain The One.

Its upper part is not bright, and its lower part is not obscure. Ceaseless in its action, it yet cannot be named, and then it again returns and becomes nothing. This is called the Form of the Formless, and the Semblance of the Invisible; this is called the Fleeting and Indeterminable.

We meet it and do not see its Front; we follow it, and do not see its Back. When we can lay hold of the Tao of old to direct the things of the present day, and are able to know it as it was of old in the beginning, this is called (unwinding) the clue of Tao.

CHAPTER 15

The skilful masters (of the Tao) in old times, with a subtle and exquisite penetration, comprehended its mysteries, and were deep (also) so as to elude men's knowledge. As they were thus beyond men's knowledge, I will make an effort to describe of what sort they appeared to be.

Shrinking looked they like those who wade through a stream in winter; irresolute like those who are afraid of all around them; grave like a guest (in awe of his host); evanescent like ice that is melting away; unpretentious like wood that has not been fashioned into anything; vacant like a valley, and dull like muddy water.

Who can (make) the muddy water (clear)? Let it be still, and it will gradually become clear. Who can secure the condition of rest? Let movement go on, and the condition of rest will gradually arise.

They who preserve this method of the Tao do not wish to be full (of themselves). It is through their not being full of themselves that they can afford to seem worn and not appear new and complete.

CHAPTER 16

The (state of) vacancy should be brought to the utmost degree, and that of stillness guarded with unwearying vigour. All things alike go through their processes of activity, and (then) we see them return (to their original state). When things (in the vegetable world) have displayed their luxuriant growth, we see each of them return to its root. This returning to their root is what we call the state of stillness; and that stillness may be called a reporting that they have fulfilled their appointed end.

The report of that fulfilment is the regular, unchanging rule. To know that unchanging rule is to be intelligent; not to know it leads to wild movements and evil issues. The knowledge of that unchanging rule produces a (grand) capacity and forbearance, and that capacity and forbearance lead to a community (of feeling with all things). From this community of feeling comes a kingliness of character; and he who is king-like goes on to be heaven-like. In that likeness to heaven he possesses the Tao. Possessed of the Tao, he endures long; and to the end of his bodily life, is exempt from all danger of decay.

CHAPTER 17

In the highest antiquity, (the people) did not know that there were (their rulers). In the next age they loved them and praised them. In the next they feared them; in the next they despised them. Thus it was that when faith (in the Tao) was deficient (in the rulers) a want of faith in them ensued (in the people).

How irresolute did those (earliest rulers) appear, showing (by their reticence) the importance which they set upon their words! Their work was done and their undertakings were successful, while the people all said, 'We are as we are, of ourselves!'

CHAPTER 18

When the Great Tao (Way or Method) ceased to be observed, benevolence and righteousness came into vogue. (Then) appeared wisdom and shrewdness, and there ensued great hypocrisy.

When harmony no longer prevailed throughout the six kinships, filial sons found their manifestation; when the states and clans fell into disorder, loyal ministers appeared.

CHAPTER 19

If we could renounce our sageness and discard our wisdom, it would be better for the people a hundredfold. If we could renounce our benevolence and discard our righteousness, the people would again become filial and kindly. If we could renounce our artful contrivances and discard our (scheming for) gain, there would be no thieves nor robbers.

Those three methods (of government)
Thought olden ways in elegance did fail
And made these names their want of worth to veil;
But simple views, and courses plain and true
Would selfish ends and many lusts eschew.

CHAPTER 20

When we renounce learning we have no troubles.
The (ready) 'yes,' and (flattering) 'yea;'—
Small is the difference they display.
But mark their issues, good and ill;—
What space the gulf between shall fill? What all men fear is indeed to be feared; but how wide and without end is the range of questions (asking to be discussed)!

The multitude of men look satisfied and pleased; as if enjoying a full banquet, as if mounted on a tower in spring. I alone seem listless and still, my desires having as yet given no indication of their presence. I am like an infant which has not yet smiled. I look dejected and forlorn, as if I had no home to go to. The multitude of men all have enough and to spare. I alone seem to have lost everything. My mind is that of a stupid man; I am in a state of chaos. Ordinary men look bright and intelligent, while I alone seem to be benighted. They look full of discrimination, while I alone am dull and confused. I seem to be carried about as on the sea, drifting as if I had nowhere to rest. All men have their spheres of action, while I alone seem dull and incapable, like a rude borderer. (Thus) I alone am different from other men, but I value the nursing-mother (the Tao).

CHAPTER 21

The grandest forms of active force
From Tao come, their only source.
Who can of Tao the nature tell?
Our sight it flies, our touch as well.
Eluding sight, eluding touch,
The forms of things all in it crouch;
Eluding touch, eluding sight,
There are their semblances, all right.
Profound it is, dark and obscure;
Things' essences all there endure.
Those essences the truth enfold
Of what, when seen, shall then be told.
Now it is so; 'twas so of old.
Its name—what passes not away;
So, in their beautiful array,
Things form and never know decay.

How know I that it is so with all the beauties of existing things? By this (nature of the Tao).

CHAPTER 22

The partial becomes complete; the crooked, straight; the empty, full; the worn out, new. He whose (desires) are few gets them; he whose (desires) are many goes astray.

Therefore the sage holds in his embrace the one thing (of humility), and manifests it to all the world. He is free from self-display, and therefore he shines; from self-assertion, and therefore he is distinguished; from self-boasting, and therefore his merit is acknowledged; from self-complacency, and therefore he acquires superiority. It is because he is thus free from striving that therefore no one in the world is able to strive with him.

That saying of the ancients that 'the partial becomes complete' was not vainly spoken:– all real completion is comprehended under it.

CHAPTER 23

Abstaining from speech marks him who is obeying the spontaneity of his nature. A violent wind does not last for a whole morning; a sudden rain does not last for the whole day. To whom is it that these (two) things are owing? To Heaven and Earth. If Heaven and Earth cannot make such (spasmodic) acting's last long, how much less can man!

Therefore when one is making the Tao his business, those who are also pursuing it, agree with him in it, and those who are making the manifestation of its course their object agree with him in that; while even those who are failing in both these things agree with him where they fail.

Hence, those with whom he agrees as to the Tao have the happiness of attaining to it; those with whom he agrees as to its manifestation have the happiness of attaining to it; and those with whom he agrees in their failure have also the happiness of attaining (to the Tao). (But) when there is not faith sufficient (on his part), a want of faith (in him) ensues (on the part of the others).

CHAPTER 24

He who stands on his tiptoes does not stand firm; he who stretches his legs does not walk (easily). (So), he who displays himself does not shine; he who asserts his own views is not distinguished; he who vaunts himself does not find his merit acknowledged; he who is self- conceited has no superiority allowed to him. Such conditions, viewed from the standpoint of the Tao, are like remnants of food, or a tumour on the body, which all dislike. Hence those who pursue (the course) of the Tao do not adopt and allow them.

CHAPTER 25

There was something undefined and complete, coming into existence before Heaven and Earth. How still it was and formless, standing alone, and undergoing no change, reaching everywhere and in no danger (of being exhausted)! It may be regarded as the Mother of all things.

I do not know its name, and I give it the designation of the Tao (the Way or Course). Making an effort (further) to give it a name I call it The Great.

Great, it passes on (in constant flow). Passing on, it becomes remote. Having become remote, it returns. Therefore the Tao is great; Heaven is great; Earth is great; and the (sage) king is also great. In the universe there are four that are great, and the (sage) king is one of them.

Man takes his law from the Earth; the Earth takes its law from Heaven; Heaven takes its law from the Tao. The law of the Tao is its being what it is.

CHAPTER 26

Gravity is the root of lightness; stillness, the ruler of movement.

Therefore a wise prince, marching the whole day, does not go far from his baggage wagons. Although he may have brilliant prospects to look at, he quietly remains (in his proper place), indifferent to them. How should the lord of a myriad chariots carry himself lightly before the kingdom? If he do act lightly, he has lost his root (of gravity); if he proceed to active movement, he will lose his throne.

CHAPTER 27

The skilful traveller leaves no traces of his wheels or footsteps; the skilful speaker says nothing that can be found fault with or blamed; the skilful reckoner uses no tallies; the skilful closer needs no bolts or bars, while to open what he has shut will be impossible; the skilful binder uses no strings or knots, while to unloose what he has bound will be impossible. In the same way the sage is always skilful at saving men, and so he does not cast away any man; he is always skilful at saving things, and so he does not cast away anything. This is called 'Hiding the light of his procedure.'

Therefore the man of skill is a master (to be looked up to) by him who has not the skill; and he who has not the skill is the helper of (the reputation of) him who has the skill. If the one did not honour his master, and the other did not rejoice in his helper, an (observer), though intelligent, might greatly err about them. This is called 'The utmost degree of mystery.'

CHAPTER 28

Who knows his manhood's strength,
Yet still his female feebleness maintains;
As to one channel flow the many drains,
All come to him, yea, all beneath the sky.
Thus he the constant excellence retains;
The simple child again, free from all stains.

Who knows how white attracts,
Yet always keeps himself within black's shade,
The pattern of humility displayed,
Displayed in view of all beneath the sky;
He in the unchanging excellence arrayed,
Endless return to man's first state has made.

Who knows how glory shines,
Yet loves disgrace, nor e'er for it is pale;
Behold his presence in a spacious vale,
To which men come from all beneath the sky.
The unchanging excellence completes its tale;
The simple infant man in him we hail.

The unwrought material, when divided and distributed, forms vessels. The sage, when employed, becomes the Head of all the Officers (of government); and in his greatest regulations he employs no violent measures.

CHAPTER 29

If anyone should wish to get the kingdom for himself, and to effect this by what he does, I see that he will not succeed. The kingdom is a spirit-like thing, and cannot be got by active doing. He who would so win it destroys it; he who would hold it in his grasp loses it.

The course and nature of things is such that
What was in front is now behind;
What warmed anon we freezing find.
Strength is of weakness of the spoil;
The store in ruins mocks our toil. Hence the sage puts away excessive effort, extravagance, and easy indulgence.

CHAPTER 30

He who would assist a lord of men in harmony with the Tao will not assert his mastery in the kingdom by force of arms. Such a course is sure to meet with its proper return.

Wherever a host is stationed, briars and thorns spring up. In the sequence of great armies there are sure to be bad years.

A skilful (commander) strikes a decisive blow, and stops. He does not dare (by continuing his operations) to assert and complete his mastery. He will strike the blow, but will be on his guard against being vain or boastful or arrogant in consequence of it. He strikes it as a matter of necessity; he strikes it, but not from a wish for mastery.

When things have attained their strong maturity they become old. This may be said to be not in accordance with the Tao: and what is not in accordance with it soon comes to an end.

CHAPTER 31

Now arms, however beautiful, are instruments of evil omen, hateful, it may be said, to all creatures. Therefore they who have the Tao do not like to employ them.

The superior man ordinarily considers the left hand the most honourable place, but in time of war the right hand. Those sharp weapons are instruments of evil omen, and not the instruments of the superior man;—he uses them only on the compulsion of necessity. Calm and repose are what he prizes; victory (by force of arms) is to him undesirable. To consider this desirable would be to delight in the slaughter of men; and he who delights in the slaughter of men cannot get his will in the kingdom.

On occasions of festivity to be on the left hand is the prized position; on occasions of mourning, the right hand. The second in command of the army has his place on the left; the general commanding in chief has his on the right;—his place, that is, is assigned to him as in the rites of mourning. He who has killed multitudes of men should weep for them with the bitterest grief; and the victor in battle has his place (rightly) according to those rites.

CHAPTER 32

The Tao, considered as unchanging, has no name.

Though in its primordial simplicity it may be small, the whole world dares not deal with (one embodying) it as a minister. If a feudal prince or the king could guard and hold it, all would spontaneously submit themselves to him.

Heaven and Earth (under its guidance) unite together and send down the sweet dew, which, without the directions of men, reaches equally everywhere as of its own accord.

As soon as it proceeds to action, it has a name. When it once has that name, (men) can know to rest in it. When they know to rest in it, they can be free from all risk of failure and error.

The relation of the Tao to all the world is like that of the great rivers and seas to the streams from the valleys.

CHAPTER 33

He who knows other men is discerning; he who knows himself is intelligent. He who overcomes others is strong; he who overcomes himself is mighty. He who is satisfied with his lot is rich; he who goes on acting with energy has a (firm) will.

He who does not fail in the requirements of his position, continues long; he who dies and yet does not perish, has longevity.

CHAPTER 34

All-pervading is the Great Tao! It may be found on the left hand and on the right.

All things depend on it for their production, which it gives to them, not one refusing obedience to it. When its work is accomplished, it does not claim the name of having done it. It clothes all things as with a garment, and makes no assumption of being their lord;—it may be named in the smallest things. All things return (to their root and disappear), and do not know that it is it which presides over their doing so;—it may be named in the greatest things.

Hence the sage is able (in the same way) to accomplish his great achievements. It is through his not making himself great that he can accomplish them.

CHAPTER 35

To him who holds in his hands the Great Image (of the invisible Tao), the whole world repairs. Men resort to him, and receive no hurt, but (find) rest, peace, and the feeling of ease.

Music and dainties will make the passing guest stop (for a time). But though the Tao as it comes from the mouth, seems insipid and has no flavour, though it seems not worth being looked at or listened to, the use of it is inexhaustible.

CHAPTER 36

When one is about to take an inspiration, he is sure to make a (previous) expiration; when he is going to weaken another, he will first strengthen him; when he is going to overthrow another, he will first have raised him up; when he is going to despoil another, he will first have made gifts to him:—this is called 'Hiding the light (of his procedure).'

The soft overcomes the hard; and the weak the strong.

Fishes should not be taken from the deep; instruments for the profit of a state should not be shown to the people.

CHAPTER 37

The Tao in its regular course does nothing (for the sake of doing it), and so there is nothing which it does not do.

If princes and kings were able to maintain it, all things would of themselves be transformed by them.

If this transformation became to me an object of desire, I would express the desire by the nameless simplicity.

Simplicity without a name
Is free from all external aim.
With no desire, at rest and still,
All things go right as of their will.

PART 2

CHAPTER 38

(Those who) possessed in highest degree the attributes (of the Tao) did not (seek) to show them, and therefore they possessed them (in fullest measure). (Those who) possessed in a lower degree those attributes (sought how) not to lose them, and therefore they did not possess them (in fullest measure).

(Those who) possessed in the highest degree those attributes did nothing (with a purpose), and had no need to do anything. (Those who) possessed them in a lower degree were (always) doing, and had need to be so doing.

(Those who) possessed the highest benevolence were (always seeking) to carry it out, and had no need to be doing so. (Those who) possessed the highest righteousness were (always seeking) to carry it out, and had need to be so doing.

(Those who) possessed the highest (sense of) propriety were (always seeking) to show it, and when men did not respond to it, they bared the arm and marched up to them.

Thus it was that when the Tao was lost, its attributes appeared; when its attributes were lost, benevolence appeared; when benevolence was lost, righteousness appeared; and when righteousness was lost, the proprieties appeared.

Now propriety is the attenuated form of leal-heartedness and good faith, and is also the commencement of disorder; swift apprehension is (only) a flower of the Tao, and is the beginning of stupidity.

Thus it is that the Great man abides by what is solid, and eschews what is flimsy; dwells with the fruit and not with the flower. It is thus that he puts away the one and makes choice of the other.

CHAPTER 39

The things which form of old have got the One (the Tao) are—

Heaven which by it is bright and pure;
Earth rendered thereby firm and sure;
Spirits with powers by it supplied;
Valleys kept full throughout their void
All creatures which through it do live
Princes and kings who from it get
The model which to all they give. All these are the results of the One (Tao).

If heaven were not thus pure, it soon would rend;
If earth were not thus sure, 'twould break and bend;
Without these powers, the spirits soon would fail;
If not so filled, the drought would parch each vale;
Without that life, creatures would pass away;
Princes and kings, without that moral sway,
However grand and high, would all decay.

Thus it is that dignity finds its (firm) root in its (previous) meanness, and what is lofty finds its stability in the lowness (from which it rises). Hence princes and kings call themselves 'Orphans,' 'Men of small virtue,' and as 'Carriages without a nave.'

Is not this an acknowledgment that in their considering themselves mean they see the foundation of their dignity? So it is that in the enumeration of the different parts of a carriage we do not come on what makes it answer the ends of a carriage. They do not wish to show themselves elegant-looking as jade, but (prefer) to be coarse-looking as an (ordinary) stone.

CHAPTER 40

The movement of the Tao
By contraries proceeds;
And weakness marks the course
Of Tao's mighty deeds.

All things under heaven sprang from It as existing (and named); that existence sprang from It as non-existent (and not named).

CHAPTER 41

Scholars of the highest class, when they hear about the Tao, earnestly carry it into practice. Scholars of the middle class, when they have heard about it, seem now to keep it and now to lose it. Scholars of the lowest class, when they have heard about it, laugh greatly at it. If it were not (thus) laughed at, it would not be fit to be the Tao.

Therefore the sentence-makers have thus expressed themselves:—

'The Tao, when brightest seen, seems light to lack;
Who progress in it makes, seems drawing back;
It's even way is like a rugged track.
Its highest virtue from the vale doth rise;
Its greatest beauty seems to offend the eyes;
And he has most whose lot the least supplies.
Its firmest virtue seems but poor and low;
Its solid truth seems change to undergo;
Its largest square doth yet no corner show
A vessel great, it is the slowest made;
Loud is its sound, but never word it said;
A semblance great, the shadow of a shade.'

The Tao is hidden, and has no name; but it is the Tao which is skilful at imparting (to all things what they need) and making them complete.

CHAPTER 42

The Tao produced One; One produced Two; Two produced Three; Three produced All things. All things leave behind them the Obscurity (out of which they have come), and go forward to embrace the Brightness (into which they have emerged), while they are harmonised by the Breath of Vacancy.

What men dislike is to be orphans, to have little virtue, to be as carriages without naves; and yet these are the designations which kings and princes use for themselves. So it is that some things are increased by being diminished, and others are diminished by being increased.

What other men (thus) teach, I also teach. The violent and strong do not die their natural death. I will make this the basis of my teaching.

CHAPTER 43

The softest thing in the world dashes against and overcomes the hardest; that which has no (substantial) existence enters where there is no crevice. I know hereby what advantage belongs to doing nothing (with a purpose).

There are few in the world who attain to the teaching without words, and the advantage arising from non-action.

CHAPTER 44

Or fame or life,
Which do you hold more dear?
Or life or wealth,
To which would you adhere?
Keep life and lose those other things;
Keep them and lose your life:—which brings
Sorrow and pain more near?

Thus we may see,
Who cleaves to fame
Rejects what is more great;
Who loves large stores
Gives up the richer state.

Who is content
Needs fear no shame.
Who knows to stop
Incurs no blame.
From danger free
Long live shall he.

CHAPTER 45

Who thinks his great achievements poor
Shall find his vigour long endure.
Of greatest fulness, deemed a void,
Exhaustion ne'er shall stem the tide.
Do thou what's straight still crooked deem;
Thy greatest art still stupid seem,
And eloquence a stammering scream.

Constant action overcomes cold; being still overcomes heat. Purity and stillness give the correct law to all under heaven.

CHAPTER 46

When the Tao prevails in the world, they send back their swift horses to (draw) the dung-carts. When the Tao is disregarded in the world, the war-horses breed in the border lands.

There is no guilt greater than to sanction ambition; no calamity greater than to be discontented with one's lot; no fault greater than the wish to be getting. Therefore the sufficiency of contentment is an enduring and unchanging sufficiency.

CHAPTER 47

Without going outside his door, one understands (all that takes place) under the sky; without looking out from his window, one sees the Tao of Heaven. The farther that one goes out (from himself), the less he knows.

Therefore the sages got their knowledge without travelling; gave their (right) names to things without seeing them; and accomplished their ends without any purpose of doing so.

CHAPTER 48

He who devotes himself to learning (seeks) from day to day to increase (his knowledge); he who devotes himself to the Tao (seeks) from day to day to diminish (his doing).

He diminishes it and again diminishes it, till he arrives at doing nothing (on purpose). Having arrived at this point of non-action, there is nothing which he does not do.

He who gets as his own all under heaven does so by giving himself no trouble (with that end). If one take trouble (with that end), he is not equal to getting as his own all under heaven.

CHAPTER 49

The sage has no invariable mind of his own; he makes the mind of the people his mind.

To those who are good (to me), I am good; and to those who are not good (to me), I am also good;—and thus (all) get to be good. To those who are sincere (with me), I am sincere; and to those who are not sincere (with me), I am also sincere;—and thus (all) get to be sincere.

The sage has in the world an appearance of indecision, and keeps his mind in a state of indifference to all. The people all keep their eyes and ears directed to him, and he deals with them all as his children.

CHAPTER 50

Men come forth and live; they enter (again) and die.

Of every ten three are ministers of life (to themselves); and three are ministers of death.

There are also three in every ten whose aim is to live, but whose movements tend to the land (or place) of death. And for what reason? Because of their excessive endeavours to perpetuate life.

But I have heard that he who is skilful in managing the life entrusted to him for a time travels on the land without having to shun rhinoceros or tiger, and enters a host without having to avoid buff coat or sharp weapon. The rhinoceros finds no place in him into which to thrust its horn, nor the tiger a place in which to fix its claws, nor the weapon a place to admit its point. And for what reason? Because there is in him no place of death.

CHAPTER 51

All things are produced by the Tao, and nourished by its out flowing operation. They receive their forms according to the nature of each, and are completed according to the circumstances of their condition. Therefore all things without exception honour the Tao, and exalt its out flowing operation.

This honouring of the Tao and exalting of its operation is not the result of any ordination, but always a spontaneous tribute.

Thus it is that the Tao produces (all things), nourishes them, brings them to their full growth, nurses them, completes them, matures them, maintains them, and overspreads them.

It produces them and makes no claim to the possession of them; it carries them through their processes and does not vaunt its ability in doing so; it brings them to maturity and exercises no control over them;—this is called its mysterious operation.

CHAPTER 52

(The Tao) which originated all under the sky is to be considered as the mother of them all.

When the mother is found, we know what her children should be. When one knows that he is his mother's child, and proceeds to guard (the qualities of) the mother that belong to him, to the end of his life he will be free from all peril.

Let him keep his mouth closed, and shut up the portals (of his nostrils), and all his life he will be exempt from laborious exertion. Let him keep his mouth open, and (spend his breath) in the promotion of his affairs, and all his life there will be no safety for him.

The perception of what is small is (the secret of clear- sightedness; the guarding of what is soft and tender is (the secret of) strength.

Who uses well his light,
Reverting to its (source so) bright,
Will from his body ward all blight,
And hides the unchanging from men's sight.

CHAPTER 53

If I were suddenly to become known, and (put into a position to) conduct (a government) according to the Great Tao, what I should be most afraid of would be a boastful display.

The great Tao (or way) is very level and easy; but people love the by-ways.

Their court(-yards and buildings) shall be well kept, but their fields shall be ill-cultivated, and their granaries very empty. They shall wear elegant and ornamented robes, carry a sharp sword at their girdle, pamper themselves in eating and drinking, and have a superabundance of property and wealth;—such (princes) may be called robbers and boasters. This is contrary to the Tao surely!

CHAPTER 54

What (Tao's) skilful planter plants
Can never be uptorn;
What his skilful arms enfold,
From him can ne'er be borne.
Sons shall bring in lengthening line,
Sacrifices to his shrine.

Tao when nursed within one's self,
His vigour will make true;
And where the family it rules
What riches will accrue!
The neighbourhood where it prevails
In thriving will abound;
And when 'tis seen throughout the state,
Good fortune will be found.
Employ it the kingdom o'er,
And men thrive all around.

In this way the effect will be seen in the person, by the observation of different cases; in the family; in the neighbourhood; in the state; and in the kingdom.

How do I know that this effect is sure to hold thus all under the sky? By this (method of observation).

CHAPTER 55

He who has in himself abundantly the attributes (of the Tao) is like an infant. Poisonous insects will not sting him; fierce beasts will not seize him; birds of prey will not strike him.

(The infant's) bones are weak and its sinews soft, but yet its grasp is firm. It knows not yet the union of male and female, and yet its virile member may be excited;—showing the perfection of its physical essence. All day long it will cry without its throat becoming hoarse;—showing the harmony (in its constitution).

To him by whom this harmony is known,
(The secret of) the unchanging (Tao) is shown,
And in the knowledge wisdom finds its throne.
All life-increasing arts to evil turn;
Where the mind makes the vital breath to burn,
(False) is the strength, (and o'er it we should mourn.)

When things have become strong, they (then) become old, which may be said to be contrary to the Tao. Whatever is contrary to the Tao soon ends.

CHAPTER 56

He who knows (the Tao) does not (care to) speak (about it); he who is (ever ready to) speak about it does not know it.

He (who knows it) will keep his mouth shut and close the portals (of his nostrils). He will blunt his sharp points and unravel the complications of things; he will attemper his brightness, and bring himself into agreement with the obscurity (of others). This is called 'the Mysterious Agreement.'

(Such an one) cannot be treated familiarly or distantly; he is beyond all consideration of profit or injury; of nobility or meanness:—he is the noblest man under heaven.

CHAPTER 57

A state may be ruled by (measures of) correction; weapons of war may be used with crafty dexterity; (but) the kingdom is made one's own (only) by freedom from action and purpose.

How do I know that it is so? By these facts:— In the kingdom the multiplication of prohibitive enactments increases the poverty of the people; the more implements to add to their profit that the people have, the greater disorder is there in the state and clan; the more acts of crafty dexterity that men possess, the more do strange contrivances appear; the more display there is of legislation, the more thieves and robbers there are.

Therefore a sage has said, 'I will do nothing (of purpose), and the people will be transformed of themselves; I will be fond of keeping still, and the people will of themselves become correct. I will take no trouble about it, and the people will of themselves become rich; I will manifest no ambition, and the people will of themselves attain to the primitive simplicity.'

CHAPTER 58

The government that seems the most unwise,
Oft goodness to the people best supplies;
That which is meddling, touching everything,
Will work but ill, and disappointment bring. Misery!—happiness is to be found by its side! Happiness!—misery lurks beneath it! Who knows what either will come to in the end?

Shall we then dispense with correction? The (method of) correction shall by a turn become distortion, and the good in it shall by a turn become evil. The delusion of the people (on this point) has indeed subsisted for a long time.

Therefore the sage is (like) a square which cuts no one (with its angles); (like) a corner which injures no one (with its sharpness). He is straightforward, but allows himself no license; he is bright, but does not dazzle.

CHAPTER 59

For regulating the human (in our constitution) and rendering the (proper) service to the heavenly, there is nothing like moderation.

It is only by this moderation that there is effected an early return (to man's normal state). That early return is what I call the repeated accumulation of the attributes (of the Tao). With that repeated accumulation of those attributes, there comes the subjugation (of every obstacle to such return). Of this subjugation we know not what shall be the limit; and when one knows not what the limit shall be, he may be the ruler of a state.

He who possesses the mother of the state may continue long. His case is like that (of the plant) of which we say that its roots are deep and its flower stalks firm:—this is the way to secure that its enduring life shall long be seen.

CHAPTER 60

Governing a great state is like cooking small fish.

Let the kingdom be governed according to the Tao, and the manes of the departed will not manifest their spiritual energy. It is not that those manes have not that spiritual energy, but it will not be employed to hurt men. It is not that it could not hurt men, but neither does the ruling sage hurt them.

When these two do not injuriously affect each other, their good influences converge in the virtue (of the Tao).

CHAPTER 61

What makes a great state is its being (like) a low-lying, down-flowing (stream);—it becomes the centre to which tend (all the small states) under heaven.

(To illustrate from) the case of all females:—the female always overcomes the male by her stillness. Stillness may be considered (a sort of) abasement.

Thus it is that a great state, by condescending to small states, gains them for itself; and that small states, by abasing themselves to a great state, win it over to them. In the one case the abasement leads to gaining adherents, in the other case to procuring favour.

The great state only wishes to unite men together and nourish them; a small state only wishes to be received by, and to serve, the other. Each gets what it desires, but the great state must learn to abase itself.

CHAPTER 62

Tao has of all things the most honoured place.
No treasures give good men so rich a grace;
Bad men it guards, and doth their ill efface.

(Its) admirable words can purchase honour; (its) admirable deeds can raise their performer above others. Even men who are not good are not abandoned by it.

Therefore when the sovereign occupies his place as the Son of Heaven, and he has appointed his three ducal ministers, though (a prince) were to send in a round symbol-of-rank large enough to fill both the hands, and that as the precursor of the team of horses (in the court-yard), such an offering would not be equal to (a lesson of) this Tao, which one might present on his knees.

Why was it that the ancients prized this Tao so much? Was it not because it could be got by seeking for it, and the guilty could escape (from the stain of their guilt) by it? This is the reason why all under heaven consider it the most valuable thing.

CHAPTER 63

(It is the way of the Tao) to act without (thinking of) acting; to conduct affairs without (feeling the) trouble of them; to taste without discerning any flavour; to consider what is small as great, and a few as many; and to recompense injury with kindness.

(The master of it) anticipates things that are difficult while they are easy, and does things that would become great while they are small. All difficult things in the world are sure to arise from a previous state in which they were easy, and all great things from one in which they were small. Therefore the sage, while he never does what is great, is able on that account to accomplish the greatest things.

He who lightly promises is sure to keep but little faith; he who is continually thinking things easy is sure to find them difficult. Therefore the sage sees difficulty even in what seems easy, and so never has any difficulties.

CHAPTER 64

That which is at rest is easily kept hold of; before a thing has given indications of its presence, it is easy to take measures against it; that which is brittle is easily broken; that which is very small is easily dispersed. Action should be taken before a thing has made its appearance; order should be secured before disorder has begun.

The tree which fills the arms grew from the tiniest sprout; the tower of nine storeys rose from a (small) heap of earth; the journey of a thousand li commenced with a single step.

He who acts (with an ulterior purpose) does harm; he who takes hold of a thing (in the same way) loses his hold. The sage does not act (so), and therefore does no harm; he does not lay hold (so), and therefore does not lose his bold. (But) people in their conduct of affairs are constantly ruining them when they are on the eve of success. If they were careful at the end, as (they should be) at the beginning, they would not so ruin them.

Therefore the sage desires what (other men) do not desire, and does not prize things difficult to get; he learns what (other men) do not learn, and turns back to what the multitude of men have passed by. Thus he helps the natural development of all things, and does not dare to act (with an ulterior purpose of his own).

CHAPTER 65

The ancients who showed their skill in practising the Tao did so, not to enlighten the people, but rather to make them simple and ignorant.

The difficulty in governing the people arises from their having much knowledge. He who (tries to) govern a state by his wisdom is a scourge to it; while he who does not (try to) do so is a blessing.

He who knows these two things finds in them also his model and rule. Ability to know this model and rule constitutes what we call the mysterious excellence (of a governor). Deep and far-reaching is such mysterious excellence, showing indeed its possessor as opposite to others, but leading them to a great conformity to him.

CHAPTER 66

That whereby the rivers and seas are able to receive the homage and tribute of all the valley streams, is their skill in being lower than they;—it is thus that they are the kings of them all. So it is that the sage (ruler), wishing to be above men, puts himself by his words below them, and, wishing to be before them, places his person behind them.

In this way though he has his place above them, men do not feel his weight, nor though he has his place before them, do they feel it an injury to them.

Therefore all in the world delight to exalt him and do not weary of him. Because he does not strive, no one finds it possible to strive with him.

CHAPTER 67

All the world says that, while my Tao is great, it yet appears to be inferior (to other systems of teaching). Now it is just its greatness that makes it seem to be inferior. If it were like any other (system), for long would its smallness have been known!

But I have three precious things which I prize and hold fast. The first is gentleness; the second is economy; and the third is shrinking from taking precedence of others.

With that gentleness I can be bold; with that economy I can be liberal; shrinking from taking precedence of others, I can become a vessel of the highest honour. Now-a-days they give up gentleness and are all for being bold; economy, and are all for being liberal; the hindmost place, and seek only to be foremost;—(of all which the end is) death.

Gentleness is sure to be victorious even in battle, and firmly to maintain its ground. Heaven will save its possessor, by his (very) gentleness protecting him.

CHAPTER 68

He who in (Tao's) wars has skill
Assumes no martial port;
He who fights with most good will
To rage makes no resort.
He who vanquishes yet still
Keeps from his foes apart;
He whose hests men most fulfil
Yet humbly plies his art.

Thus we say, 'He ne'er contends,
And therein is his might.'
Thus we say, 'Men's wills he bends,
That they with him unite.'
Thus we say, 'Like Heaven's his ends,
No sage of old more bright.'

CHAPTER 69

A master of the art of war has said, 'I do not dare to be the host (to commence the war); I prefer to be the guest (to act on the defensive). I do not dare to advance an inch; I prefer to retire a foot.' This is called marshalling the ranks where there are no ranks; baring the arms (to fight) where there are no arms to bare; grasping the weapon where there is no weapon to grasp; advancing against the enemy where there is no enemy.

There is no calamity greater than lightly engaging in war. To do that is near losing (the gentleness) which is so precious. Thus it is that when opposing weapons are (actually) crossed, he who deplores (the situation) conquers.

CHAPTER 70

My words are very easy to know, and very easy to practise; but there is no one in the world who is able to know and able to practise them.

There is an originating and all-comprehending (principle) in my words, and an authoritative law for the things (which I enforce). It is because they do not know these, that men do not know me.

They who know me are few, and I am on that account (the more) to be prized. It is thus that the sage wears (a poor garb of) hair cloth, while he carries his (signet of) jade in his bosom.

CHAPTER 71

To know and yet (think) we do not know is the highest (attainment); not to know (and yet think) we do know is a disease.

It is simply by being pained at (the thought of) having this disease that we are preserved from it. The sage has not the disease. He knows the pain that would be inseparable from it, and therefore he does not have it.

CHAPTER 72

When the people do not fear what they ought to fear, that which is their great dread will come on them.

Let them not thoughtlessly indulge themselves in their ordinary life; let them not act as if weary of what that life depends on.

It is by avoiding such indulgence that such weariness does not arise.

Therefore the sage knows (these things) of himself, but does not parade (his knowledge); loves, but does not (appear to set a) value on, himself. And thus he puts the latter alternative away and makes choice of the former.

CHAPTER 73

He whose boldness appears in his daring (to do wrong, in defiance of the laws) is put to death; he whose boldness appears in his not daring (to do so) lives on. Of these two cases the one appears to be advantageous, and the other to be injurious. But

When Heaven's anger smites a man,
Who the cause shall truly scan? On this account the sage feels a difficulty (as to what to do in the former case).

It is the way of Heaven not to strive, and yet it skilfully overcomes; not to speak, and yet it is skilful in (obtaining a reply; does not call, and yet men come to it of themselves. Its demonstrations are quiet, and yet its plans are skilful and effective. The meshes of the net of Heaven are large; far apart, but letting nothing escape.

CHAPTER 74

The people do not fear death; to what purpose is it to (try to) frighten them with death? If the people were always in awe of death, and I could always seize those who do wrong, and put them to death, who would dare to do wrong?

There is always One who presides over the infliction death. He who would inflict death in the room of him who so presides over it may be described as hewing wood instead of a great carpenter. Seldom is it that he who undertakes the hewing, instead of the great carpenter, does not cut his own hands!

CHAPTER 75

The people suffer from famine because of the multitude of taxes consumed by their superiors. It is through this that they suffer famine.

The people are difficult to govern because of the (excessive) agency of their superiors (in governing them). It is through this that they are difficult to govern.

The people make light of dying because of the greatness of their labours in seeking for the means of living. It is this which makes them think light of dying. Thus it is that to leave the subject of living altogether out of view is better than to set a high value on it.

CHAPTER 76

Man at his birth is supple and weak; at his death, firm and strong. (So it is with) all things. Trees and plants, in their early growth, are soft and brittle; at their death, dry and withered.

Thus it is that firmness and strength are the concomitants of death; softness and weakness, the concomitants of life.

Hence he who (relies on) the strength of his forces does not conquer; and a tree which is strong will fill the out-stretched arms, (and thereby invites the feller.)

Therefore the place of what is firm and strong is below, and that of what is soft and weak is above.

CHAPTER 77

May not the Way (or Tao) of Heaven be compared to the (method of) bending a bow? The (part of the bow) which was high is brought low, and what was low is raised up. (So Heaven) diminishes where there is superabundance, and supplements where there is deficiency.

It is the Way of Heaven to diminish superabundance, and to supplement deficiency. It is not so with the way of man. He takes away from those who have not enough to add to his own superabundance.

Who can take his own superabundance and therewith serve all under heaven? Only he who is in possession of the Tao!

Therefore the (ruling) sage acts without claiming the results as his; he achieves his merit and does not rest (arrogantly) in it:—he does not wish to display his superiority.

CHAPTER 78

There is nothing in the world more soft and weak than water, and yet for attacking things that are firm and strong there is nothing that can take precedence of it;—for there is nothing (so effectual) for which it can be changed.

Everyone in the world knows that the soft overcomes the hard, and the weak the strong, but no one is able to carry it out in practice.

Therefore a sage has said,
'He who accepts his state's reproach,
Is hailed therefore its altars' lord;
To him who bears men's direful woes
They all the name of King accord.'

Words that are strictly true seem to be paradoxical.

CHAPTER 79

When a reconciliation is effected (between two parties) after a great animosity, there is sure to be a grudge remaining (in the mind of the one who was wrong). And how can this be beneficial (to the other)?

Therefore (to guard against this), the sage keeps the left-hand portion of the record of the engagement, and does not insist on the (speedy) fulfilment of it by the other party. (So), he who has the attributes (of the Tao) regards (only) the conditions of the engagement, while he who has not those attributes regards only the conditions favourable to himself.

In the Way of Heaven, there is no partiality of love; it is always on the side of the good man.

CHAPTER 80

In a little state with a small population, I would so order it, that, though there were individuals with the abilities of ten or a hundred men, there should be no employment of them; I would make the people, while looking on death as a grievous thing, yet not remove elsewhere (to avoid it).

Though they had boats and carriages, they should have no occasion to ride in them; though they had buff coats and sharp weapons, they should have no occasion to don or use them.

I would make the people return to the use of knotted cords (instead of the written characters).

They should think their (coarse) food sweet; their (plain) clothes beautiful; their (poor) dwellings places of rest; and their common (simple) ways sources of enjoyment.

There should be a neighbouring state within sight, and the voices of the fowls and dogs should be heard all the way from it to us, but I would make the people to old age, even to death, not have any intercourse with it.

CHAPTER 81

Sincere words are not fine; fine words are not sincere. Those who are skilled (in the Tao) do not dispute (about it); the disputatious are not skilled in it. Those who know (the Tao) are not extensively learned; the extensively learned do not know it.

The sage does not accumulate (for himself). The more that he expends for others, the more does he possess of his own; the more that he gives to others, the more does he have himself.

With all the sharpness of the Way of Heaven, it injures not; with all the doing in the way of the sage he does not strive.

OTHER HARDBACK BOOKS

- 1984 by George Orwell
  Fiction/Classics, ISBN: 9788193545836
- Abraham Lincoln by Lord Charnwood
  Biographies/Leaders, ISBN: 9789387669147
- Alice's Adventures in Wonderland by Lewis Carroll
  Children's/Classics, ISBN: 9789387669055
- Animal Farm by George Orwell
  Fiction/Classics, ISBN: 9789387669062
- Anthem by Ayn Rand
  Fiction/Classics, ISBN: 9789389157178
- As a Man Thinketh by James Allen
  Fiction/Classics, ISBN: 9789388118422
- Awakened Imagination by Neville Goddard
  Religion & Spirituality, ISBN: 9789389157185
- Be What You Wish by Neville Goddard
  Mind, Body & Spirit, ISBN: 9789388118163
- Becoming a Writer by Dorothea Brande
  Self Help/General, ISBN: 9789389157192
- Believe in Yourself by Joseph Murphy
  Mind, Body & Spirit, ISBN: 9789388118439
- Black Beauty by Anna Sewell
  Children's/Classics, ISBN: 9789388118262
- Civilization and Its Discontents by Sigmund Freud
  Social Sciences/General, ISBN: 9789388118279
- Demian by Hermann Hesse
  Fiction/Classics, ISBN: 9789388118170
- Feeling is the Secret by Neville Goddard
  Religion & Spirituality, ISBN: 9789389157208

Search the book by its ISBN

OTHER HARDBACK BOOKS

- Gitanjali by Rabindranath Tagore
  Fiction/Poems, ISBN: 9789387669079
- Great Speeches of Abraham Lincoln by Abraham Lincoln
  History/United States, ISBN: 9789387669154
- How to Attract Money by Joseph Murphy
  Self Help/Success, ISBN: 9789388118446
- How to be Filled with the Holy Spirit by A.W. Tozer
  Religion/Christianity, ISBN: 9789389157215
- How to Enjoy Your Life and Your Job by Dale Carnegie
  Self Help/General, ISBN: 9789388118293
- Illust. Biography of William Shakespeare by Manju Gupta
  Biographies/Authors, ISBN: 9789387669246
- Madhubala by Manju Gupta
  Biographies/Cinems, ISBN: 9789387669253
- Mansarover 1 (Hindi) by Premchand
  Fiction/Short Stories, ISBN: 9789387669086
- Meditations by Marcus Aurelius
  Non Fiction/Philosopy, ISBN: 9789388118781
- My Inventions: The Autobio. of Nikola Tesla by Nikola Tesla
  Autobiographies/Scientists, ISBN: 9789388118187
- Selected Stories of Rabindranath Tagore by Rabindranath Tagore
  Fiction/Short Stories, ISBN: 9789387669307
- Sense and Sensibility by Jane Austen
  Fiction/Classics, ISBN: 9789387669109
- Siddhartha by Hermann Hesse
  Fiction/Classics, ISBN: 9789387669116
- Tales from India by Rudyard Kipling
  Fiction/Short Stories, ISBN: 9789387669123

Search the book by its ISBN

OTHER HARDBACK BOOKS

- Tales from Shakespeare by Charles Lamb, Mary Lamb
  Fiction/Short Stories, ISBN: 9789387669314
- The Alchemy of Happiness by Al-Ghazzali
  Religion & Spirituality, ISBN: 9789388118309
- The Art of Public Speaking by Dale Carnegie
  Self Help/General, ISBN: 9789388118477
- The Autobiography of a Yogi by Paramahansa Yogananda
  Autobiographies/General, ISBN: 9789387669192
- The Dynamic Laws of Prosperity by Catherine Ponder
  Mind, Body & Spirit, ISBN: 9789388118194
- The Elements of Style by William Strunk
  Non Fiction/Skill, ISBN: 9789389157222
- The Game of Life and How to Play It by Florence Scovel Shinn
  Mind, Body & Spirit, ISBN: 9789388118316
- The Imitation of Christ by Thomas À Kempis
  Religion/Christianity, ISBN: 9789388118200
- The Jungle Book by Rudyard Kipling
  Children's/Classics, ISBN: 9789387669338
- The Knowledge of the Holy by A.W. Tozer
  Religion/Christianity, ISBN: 9789389157239
- The Light of Asia by Sir Edwin Arnold
  Fiction/Poetry, ISBN: 9789387669130
- The Magic of Faith by Joseph Murphy
  Mind, Body & Spirit, ISBN: 9789388118712
- The Origin of Species by Charles Darwin
  Sciences/Life Sciences, ISBN: 9789387669345
- The Path of Prosperity by James Allen
  Mind, Body & Spirit, ISBN: 9789388118323

Search the book by its ISBN

OTHER HARDBACK BOOKS

- The Power of Awareness by Neville Goddard
  Mind, Body & Spirit, ISBN: 9789388118330
- The Power of Concentration by Theron Q. Dumont
  Self Help/General, ISBN: 9789388118224
- The Power of Positive Thinking by Norman Vincent Peale
  Mind, Body & Spirit, ISBN: 9789388118729
- The Prophet by Kahlil Gibran
  Fiction/Classics, ISBN: 9789388118453
- The Psychopathology of Everyday Life by Sigmund Freud
  Non Fiction/Psychology, ISBN: 9789388118231
- The Pursuit of God by A.W. Tozer
  Religion/Christianity, ISBN: 9789389157246
- The Quick and Easy Way to Effec. Speaking by Dale Carnegie
  Self Help/General, ISBN: 9789388118347
- The Science of Getting Rich by Wallace D. Wattles
  Self Help/Success, ISBN: 9789387669239
- The Seven Laws of Teaching by John Milton Gregory
  Self Help/General, ISBN: 9789388118460
- The Upanishads by Swami Paramananda
  Religion/Hinduism, ISBN: 9789388118774
- The World as I See It by Albert Einstein
  Non Fiction/Philosopy, ISBN: 9789388118248
- Thought Vibration by William Walker Atkinson
  Non Fiction/Philosopy, ISBN: 9789389157253
- Wake Up and Live! by Dorothea Brande
  Mind, Body & Spirit, ISBN: 9789388118255
- Your Faith is Your Fortune by Neville Goddard
  Religion & Spirituality, ISBN: 9789389157260

Search the book by its ISBN